D1648170

TURN TO THE
Cross

"How often we pray, 'Lord, show me the way!' This wonderful booklet can serve to do just that as you walk in faith this holy season. It is a roadmap, a compass, and a companion all at once. Each day's brief devotion will bring you a little more deeply into communion with Christ, the hope and destination of our faith."

Bishop William Wack, CSC
Diocese of Pensacola–Tallahassee

"The simplicity of these devotionals makes them incredibly user-friendly while also being deeply thought-provoking and hugely helpful in praying through the Church's high seasons. For the daily Mass goer or the casual Christian or the intrepid questioner, these are wonderful!"

Katie Prejean McGrady
Host of the *Ave Explores* podcast and
The Katie McGrady Show on SiriusXM's The Catholic Channel

TURN TO THE
Cross

DAILY PRAYERS
FOR *Lent* AND *Holy Week* 2024

WRITTEN BY JOSH NOEM

AVE MARIA PRESS AVE Notre Dame, Indiana

Nihil Obstat: Reverend Monsignor Michael Heintz, PhD
Censor Librorum

Imprimatur: Most Reverend Kevin C. Rhoades
Bishop of Fort Wayne–South Bend
Given at Fort Wayne, Indiana, on April 26, 2023

Writer
Josh Noem

Founded in 1865, Ave Maria Press is a ministry of the United States Province of Holy Cross.

www.avemariapress.com

Paperback: ISBN-13 978-1-64680-263-0

E-book: ISBN-13 978-1-64680-264-7

Cover image © LinaraArtPrints, www.etsy.com/shop/LinaraArtPrints.

Cover and text design by Katherine Robinson.

Printed and bound in the United States of America.

WELCOME TO AVE DEVOTIONALS

Thousands of Catholics are holding this booklet in their hands, just as you are. Is it too strange to think that these words can connect us all in a meaningful way? Thank you for joining hands with us as we pray through this holy season of preparation together.

Ave Maria Press is one of the oldest continually operating Catholic publishing houses in the country. We were founded more than 150 years ago as a ministry of the Congregation of Holy Cross to honor Mary, support the spiritual needs of our everyday living, and showcase the best American Catholic writing.

Great writing has always been the backbone of Ave Maria Press, and we're proud to have shared the voices of American Catholic giants such as Dorothy Day and Henri Nouwen and Thomas Merton. And our publications support Catholics in every stage of life, whether it's a resource that helps a young couple prepare for marriage, a Bible that helps a new mother find hope in God's faithfulness, a textbook that catechizes a high schooler, or a book that changes the way you walk through the seasons of the Church year.

Though not everything we publish speaks of her explicitly, our work also honors Mary—like her, we are here to fulfill a call to bear God's Word to the world, and to help you do the same. At the heart of every Ave book, you can find a small annunciation, an invitation to let God break into our lives in a new way. The words our authors share reflect their yeses to this good news; they write to encourage you to say yes, too.

If that feels like a big ask, you're in good company. This is a question we have to answer anew every day—especially during Advent and Lent. We created these Ave Devotionals to offer daily spiritual touch points through these special seasons. With hands joined in prayer, let us lift up our hearts!

How to Use This Booklet

God himself will set me free from the hunter's snare.

This line appears over and over again in the Church's Morning Prayer during Lent—it reminds us of the central mystery of this season: God saves us.

We all wander into snares. Perhaps you feel trapped by habits of sin, dread of your own mortality, experiences of trauma, unhealthy compulsions, raw grief, or even just the drudgery of the same daily routine. When we are stuck, our world narrows to the mechanism wrapped around our leg, and it's hard to imagine how we'll ever break free.

There is good news: Jesus leads us through death to new life. Lent is a time to turn toward the crosses we face and follow him to freedom.

Our spiritual work in Lent is not self-transformation—our disciplines are not intended to make us strong enough to save ourselves or "good" enough to be worthy of God's mercy. Rather, our Lenten work is to pattern our lives more closely on Jesus who emptied himself in self-giving love. The mystery we celebrate at Easter proclaims that this kind of love leads to new and abundant life, both when our bodies die and in our day-to-day living—now.

A habit of daily prayer will sustain us as we turn toward the Cross and follow Jesus to new life. This booklet has entries for each day in Lent: use the brief reflection and morning and evening prayers to stay anchored in God's presence. Each entry begins with a line from the Church's oldest form of prayer, the Liturgy of the Hours. These devotions build week to week on themes central to the season, including the three pillars of our shared Lenten practice: prayer, fasting, and almsgiving—disciplines that make right our relationships with God, ourselves, and others, especially people on the margins.

We adore you, O Christ, and we praise you—for by your holy Cross, you have redeemed the world! May we turn toward the Cross and learn your holy way.

February 14

ASH WEDNESDAY

Return to me with your whole heart.
JOEL 2:12

When it is time for them to spawn, some coho and sockeye salmon travel 900 miles from the Pacific Ocean into Idaho. They climb more than a mile through rivers and rapids to find the stream where they hatched. The various North American salmon species vary in their migration patterns, but all are born in fresh water and then travel out to the ocean as juveniles where they can spend years feeding and growing. At some point, something changes inside them and they return to the streams where they hatched to give life to the next generation.

They find their home river through a combination of a keen sense of smell and Earth's magnetic field. Once they leave the ocean to return to fresh water, they stop eating. Their entire physiology changes over a matter of weeks as they expend every ounce of strength they have to swim upstream. Within days of spawning, they die, and their bodies replenish the soil of the watershed with important nutrients.

Every year during Lent calls us to our Source: "Return to me with your whole heart," God tells us through the prophet Joel. As with salmon, this is a journey that will require all of our resources. Change is hard. We are set in our ways, and at times our hearts are stony. To set out in a new direction—to start navigating home, this time to the Cross—requires effort, intentionality, and discipline.

Just as a salmon's final journey is one of giving its life away, so is our Lenten journey a movement toward the holy mystery of death and new life. Death is the ultimate reality we all will face someday, but even during these next six weeks we will be asked to die to ourselves as we reorient our lives to follow the source of life, Jesus Christ. Today we turn and begin moving toward the Cross. But we never journey alone—we are part of a penitent people who are hearing the same call at the same time.

Prayer for Morning

God of life, you are our source and destination. You created us for union with you and call us to return, for we have wandered. Help me to summon the strength I need today to turn my life back toward deeper communion with you and others.

Source of life, give me an urgency to respond to you today.

Traveling Question

What obstacles have gotten in the way of my relationship with God and loved ones?

Prayer for Evening

God our creator, you made us in your image and likeness. You shaped our hearts for your love, but we turn them away in pursuit of lesser things. I hear your call to return. Grow my desire for you so I might move through the coming weeks with clarity and confidence in your mercy.

Source of life, help me be honest with myself about what needs to change in my life.

February 15

Thursday after Ash Wednesday

Father, you have taught us to overcome our sins
by prayer, fasting, and works of mercy.

We work to overcome our sins not to somehow earn God's forgiveness, but to put selfishness behind us and to live differently, to live more closely aligned with the ways of Jesus. Prayer, fasting, and almsgiving are practices that train us in the ways of selfless love, to establish new pathways that lead to life.

We will fall, for none of us is perfect, but God's love is bigger than our biggest failure. We can always return. God does not keep score—all he wants is for us to keep seeking him.

Prayer for Morning

Father, you've given your Church the disciplines of prayer, fasting, and almsgiving during this season of return and repentance. Help me intentionally and thoughtfully embrace these ancient practices so I will grow in my capacity to see and love you.

God of life, call me back to you today.

Traveling Question

What part of my interior life discourages me, and how can I turn that discouragement over to God?

Prayer for Evening

Father, this Lenten journey is a long one, and I know I will meet resistance on my way. Still, you call me to imitate your Son, who fought temptation by holding fast to your love. When I feel distant from you, help me remember that your nearness has never faltered and that you wait longingly for me to return.

God of life, keep me close to you.

February 16

FRIDAY AFTER ASH WEDNESDAY

Run so as to win.
1 CORINTHIANS 9:24

Have you ever watched an Olympic track and field competition? When the starter's gun goes off, you never see a runner stroll around just happy to be there. Olympic athletes are all in. They've put too much into their training to not give their best. They know they have a limited window of opportunity to chase glory and that this is their moment.

Lent—this is *our* moment. As St. Paul urges us, let's not give half an effort—let's give it all we have.

Prayer for Morning

Everlasting Spirit, you call us to discipline our wills to imitate Jesus more perfectly. Grant me a sense of urgency and commitment in my Lenten practice for I know my time is limited, and I want to use it well. Help me give my all in faithfulness.

God of glory, help me run to you today.

Traveling Question

What things inhibit me from committing to God right now?

Prayer for Evening

Everlasting Spirit, you meet our every effort with grace. For every step I take, you carry me two. As much as I want to get my life in order, I know only you can make me whole. Grant me deeper faith and the capacity to turn my life over to you.

God of glory, carry me in your love.

February 17

SATURDAY AFTER ASH WEDNESDAY

[Lord Jesus], may your Mother, the refuge of sinners, pray for us
and gain for us your loving forgiveness.

There are so many titles for Our Lady, but Refuge of Sinners must be
one of the most comforting. When we come face-to-face with the reality
of our sinfulness and the damage it causes to ourselves and others—
that's when we need shelter. We need a place that is safe.

God is always ready for our return—and so is Mary. As our mother
in faith, we can find refuge in her embrace. Her shelter is not a way to
hide from what we've done. Rather, we find there loving encouragement
to collect ourselves, ask for forgiveness, and try again.

Prayer for Morning

Blessed Mother, you care for me as your own, and long for me when I
wander. Having stood at the foot of the Cross, you know well the cost
of sin, and always call me back to your Son. Pray for me, that I may not
lose heart on this Lenten journey.

Refuge of Sinners, pray for me today.

Traveling Question

How can I extend encouragement and mercy to others today?

Prayer for Evening

Mary our Mother, though you were without sin, you know the trials and
temptations we face. You are full of grace and eager to help me know
God's forgiveness. Help me turn to Jesus when I least feel like it—when
I've turned away from him in some way. Pray that I learn to trust his
loving mercy as much as you do.

Refuge of Sinners, help me be honest with myself.

FIRST WEEK OF LENT: GOD IS FAITHFUL

February 18

FIRST SUNDAY OF LENT

Do not be saddened this day,
for rejoicing in the LORD is your strength!
NEHEMIAH 8:10

You have a tightly bound engine thrumming inside your ribcage, a piston pumping 100,000 times a day to feed every cell in your body. Every minute, this dynamo drives more than a gallon of plasma through the 60,000 miles of blood vessels contained in your frame. This cardiac motor is about the size of your fist, a welded knot of muscle fibers humming in your core. Grab a tennis ball and squeeze it tightly—that's the strength behind every *buh-bump*. The energy it creates over the course of a day could drive a truck twenty miles.

Now, slow down and examine just one *buh-bump* at one-eighth speed—the walls of your heart expanding and drawing in a swirl of thick blood and then contracting and sending it out. In and out, in and out, in and out—a restless rhythm that powers everything from your brain to your pinky toes.

Rhythm powers so much—from our own breathing to the way our weeks unfold. As we circulate through weekdays, we are always drawn back to Sunday. Even as the first Christians were trying to make sense of the Resurrection, they put Sunday at the core. Gathering to remember Jesus rising from the dead is the oldest Christian practice.

Sunday is a day of rejoicing—Lent cannot displace the joy at the core of our lives. If we are to participate in God's love as followers of Jesus, we cannot trudge through life. Even our Lenten disciplines are colored by the joy of Sunday because we proclaim Good News with our lives. God has won the day for us. God has won every day for us.

On Sundays, we practice gratitude, wonder, and rejoicing—particularly as we gather for the Eucharist. When we go to Mass, we are drawn into God's heart and sent out to change our world. Drawn in and sent out. In and out. *Buh-bump. Buh-bump.*

Prayer for Morning

God of love, in raising Jesus from the dead, you give life to all your children. Help me live with gratitude, wonder, and joy because of this gift, especially today as I gather with your people to worship you through your Son, Christ our Lord.

God of life, draw me ever deeper into your love.

Traveling Question

What can I do today to express gratitude and joy?

Prayer for Evening

God of love, by holding us in your divine life, you show us our purpose and our hope. Help me to rest in you, to be nourished by you, to be restored by you, so that I can carry your compassion out to the other members of the Body of Christ in need of good news.

God of life, send me out with your love.

February 19

Monday of the First Week of Lent

Understand, then, that the Lord, your God, is God indeed,
the faithful God who keeps his merciful covenant down to the
thousandth generation
toward those who love him and keep his commandments.

Lent is a time to reorient ourselves to the fundamental truth that we only find meaning and hope by placing the living God at the center of our lives. Over time, we tend to wander from that center. Our Lenten practices help us right our course and turn back toward the mystery of the Cross and the living God who died there, only to rise again to new and abundant life. It is this God with whom we are joined in merciful covenant.

Though we so often break our part of the covenant by wandering into selfishness, God remains ever faithful to it and to us.

Prayer for Morning

Almighty, ever-living One, there's nothing we can offer you that you need, yet you do not stop giving to us. You keep your promise to us to bring us into the fullness of life. Thank you for your steadfast love for me, even when I turn away from it or doubt it.

Faithful God, help me trust in your mercy.

Traveling Question

What makes me doubt God's goodness?

Prayer for Evening

Everlasting God, you are the Mighty One who created the universe and holds it in being. What a gift that you care for me so tenderly, so intimately.

Faithful God, I want you at the center of my life.

February 20

TUESDAY OF THE FIRST WEEK OF LENT

You have seen how I treated the Egyptians and how I bore you up
on eagles' wings and brought you to myself.
EXODUS 19:4

The book of Exodus holds a special place in our Lenten tradition. The story of God liberating the Israelites from Egypt and walking with them through the desert for forty years before they entered the Promised Land sets a model for our forty-day journey through Lent to the Cross, and from the Cross to the Resurrection. God is by our side for every step.

Our God is one who saves. He opens a way for us when we are trapped and oppressed, even if he has to part a sea.

Prayer for Morning

Our Father, during this Lenten season, we ponder your saving work and remember your faithfulness to us, your people. I need your saving help, too, for I am wandering in a desert. Give me confidence in your protection and compassion, so that I can keep walking in faithfulness.

God of deliverance, help me hear your voice with me today.

Traveling Question

From what do I need deliverance—and how can I turn to God for help?

Prayer for Evening

Our Father, your love possesses us with tender care and you provide for our every need. When I am weary and discouraged, bear me on eagles' wings to yourself. It feels like I have so far to go, but all I really need is you, and you are closer to me than I often realize.

God of deliverance, let me rest in your love.

February 21

WEDNESDAY OF THE FIRST WEEK OF LENT

In his mercy, God sends the Holy Spirit to shine on us,
so that our lives may radiate holiness and faith.

During the Korean War, US Army chaplain Emil Kapaun was captured along with other soldiers of his battalion. They spent the winter in a prison camp with insufficient food and clothing. After dark, Kapaun would sneak around to forage for supplies to share. Despite facing brutal punishment, he continued to visit soldiers in their barracks to offer prayer and encouragement—his courage and faith a source of light. He even taunted his captors by offering Mass on Easter morning in 1951.

Kapaun died in the camp when his body succumbed to malnutrition and exposure. "Don't worry about me," he told his fellow prisoners of war before he died. "I'm going where I always wanted to go, and when I get there, I'll say a prayer for all of you." All of us, like Emil Kapaun, can shine only because of the light that we receive.

Prayer for Morning

God of light, your love illuminates our lives. Send your Spirit to me today so that I may bring your light to places that are dark.

Radiant Spirit, fill me with your life.

Traveling Question

What part of this day needs God's light?

Prayer for Evening

God of light, your truth and love cast out darkness. Help me trust your mercy that I may turn toward you without fear.

Radiant Spirit, shine on my life and make me holy.

February 22

THURSDAY OF THE FIRST WEEK OF LENT

They shall be my people, and I will be their God.
JEREMIAH 32:38

God is not distant. His fingerprints are impressed on our bones; his name is scratched in the chambers of our hearts. He did not fashion us only to walk away.

God wants more than anything to be personally and intimately part of our lives. If we can be quiet and honest enough to draw near to God, we will discover him already near to us.

The silence of your next breath is enough to invite God in. He is closer than you think. Even this desire to welcome him is an echo of God's desire for us.

Prayer for Morning

Almighty Creator, you have made us for yourself, inscribing your life within our hearts. Whenever I turn toward you, I find you nearer than I can imagine. Hear within this prayer my desire to welcome you into my life, to dwell with your Spirit.

Spirit of the living God, fill my heart with your love.

Traveling Question

What numbs or distracts my heart from recognizing God's presence with me throughout the day?

Prayer for Evening

Loving God, you created us for union with yourself. My heart is burning for you. Rather than containing this blaze to the part of my life I carve out for prayer, grant me courage to feed the rest of my life to these flames, especially the parts I want to keep hidden from you.

Spirit of the living God, let me be consumed by your fire.

13

February 23

FRIDAY OF THE FIRST WEEK OF LENT

Teacher and Savior, you have shown us your fidelity
and made us a new creation by your passion.

Jesus came to proclaim the good news of God's saving help. Through
his teaching and healing, he inaugurated the kingdom of God here on
earth. The logic of this kingdom was threatening to people in power
and they killed him for it.

But Jesus was faithful to the end. He did not renounce any of this
good news when his life was at stake—in fact, he recommitted to his
way of self-giving love. When we follow this way, Christ makes us a new
creation. That's what we're about this Lent—embracing his fidelity and
our part in building the kingdom of God here and now.

Prayer for Morning

Lord Jesus, your words and actions revealed your love for God's people.
You reveal your love for me by your healing and guidance. I know that
when I empty myself in self-giving love, you always bring me new and
abundant life. Give me strength to embrace your Cross and confidence
in your Resurrection.

Dear Savior, help me be faithful to your way.

Traveling Question

How will I experience God's kingdom breaking into my life today?

Prayer for Evening

Jesus our teacher, you were faithful to the Father right to the end of
your earthly life, and you remain faithful to me always. Your creative
love transforms me. Bring me close to you and keep me from falling
into sin. I rely on your help in this Lenten journey.

Dear Savior, make me a new creation in you.

February 24

SATURDAY OF THE FIRST WEEK OF LENT

Draw close to God, and he will draw close to you.
JAMES 4:8

Like the prodigal son, when we decide to return, we find God watching and waiting for us to come back—and running to embrace us at first sight.

In pushing away evil, we discover that goodness fills in behind it; in resisting temptation, we become stronger in our weakness. Sin looms over us like a creeping darkness, but it flees at any flicker of light. We don't have to summon that spark ourselves—the dawn of God's love has already broken over us. We simply need to turn our faces to the sun.

Prayer for Morning

God of goodness, your radiant love warms us and brings us life. When selfishness and shallow desires threaten to pull me into myself, help me return to you with humility. May my Lenten practice draw me closer to you.

Faithful Father, I give my life to you today.

Traveling Question

What can I do to resist sin today?

Prayer for Evening

God of goodness, you are both near us and beyond us. You embrace me completely yet also draw me beyond myself into deeper, fuller life. Grant me confidence in your faithfulness, even when I can't see where you are leading me, and help me resist whatever hinders my faithfulness to you.

Faithful Father, thank you for sharing your life with me.

February 25

SECOND SUNDAY OF LENT

Come now, let us set things right, says the LORD.
Though your sins be like scarlet,
they may become white as snow;
though they be red like crimson, they may become white as wool.

ISAIAH 1:18

Bruno Sserunkuuma grew up the son of a chief in Uganda in the late 1800s. As a child of privilege, he had every pleasure at his disposal. People remember him being cruel, violent, and often drunk. He also mistreated women.

His brother had a connection at the king's palace, and he secured a role for Bruno there as a page. The other servants Bruno met in the palace showed him Christian faith, and he decided to seek baptism at the age of twenty-nine. We don't know much more than that, but it's no stretch to think that his old way of living was making him miserable—that he was looking for a change. Soon, people started to notice that he was different: he mastered his temper and controlled his passions.

Bruno was given the role of gatekeeper in the palace and performed his duties well. When the king rewarded him by placing two young women in his household as his wives, Bruno slipped back into his old ways. The head page, Charles Lwanga, visited Bruno and reminded him of his baptismal promises and the dignity of the two women. In that moment, Bruno had a choice to make: was he a son of a chief, or was he a son of God? If he was son of a chief, he had a lot of living to do; if he was a son of God, there was a lot of dying ahead.

Bruno walked away, made a good confession, and changed his life again. That decision was only possible because he had confidence in

God's mercy. He decided that God's love for him was the bedrock of his identity.

When the king grew tired of the Christians and their way of life, he gathered them all together, with Charles at the head, and challenged them to renounce their faith. Bruno had already proven his worth to the king and stood at his position at the gate. He could have watched in safety, but he stepped forward to join his friends. They were bound, beaten, marched for miles, and burned alive.

We remember them as the Ugandan Martyrs, and St. Bruno as a son of God who never gave up his confidence that God's mercy is bigger than any sin, bigger than any suffering.

Prayer for Morning

God of love, your love is our only source of life. In turning away from you, we turn toward the stain of death. Help me turn toward you today with confidence that you will make me clean.

Father of mercy, call me to yourself today.

Traveling Question

What parts of my life feel stained?

Prayer for Evening

God of love, you fashioned me in your own image. When I lose sight of who I am, call me back to you and to my truest self. Give me confidence that nothing is so big as to stand in the way of your love for me.

Father of mercy, thank you for making me your beloved.

February 26

MONDAY OF THE SECOND WEEK OF LENT

God our Father, teach us to find new life through penance.
Keep us from sin, and help us live by your commandment of love.

Lent is known as a season of repentance, but what does that mean? What is penance?

Penance in Catholic understanding is not self-inflicted punishment—it is a way to change our lives. When we come back to the truth of who we are and who God is, we gain clarity about how we have wandered and a desire grows to take steps to redirect ourselves. That action is penance: voluntary self-denial in order to acknowledge our selfishness and to *correct our course*. We deny ourselves in order to increase our capacity to see and respond to the promptings of Love and thereby participate in the self-giving work of the kingdom.

Prayer for Morning

Loving God, your mercy knows no limits. As I seek to return to deeper life with you, give me honesty and courage to use penance as a tool to become more generous, hopeful, and joyful. Keep me from falling into the trap of thinking this season of Lent is all about me.

Spirit of truth and love, help me see myself clearly today.

Traveling Question

Which of my habits are incompatible with God's life?

Prayer for Evening

Loving God, you come to us as salvation—from death, from sin, from the prison of our own selfishness. Newness of life follows you wherever you go. Help me to perceive you more acutely and to follow where you are leading.

Spirit of truth and love, fill my heart.

February 27

TUESDAY OF THE SECOND WEEK OF LENT

Lord, create a new spirit within us.

Our Lenten practice is a preparation for a new life. We anticipate and prepare for the Paschal Triduum, culminating in the great feast of Easter, because the risen Christ continues to free us from the effects of sin, even death. This liberation does not mean that we will not suffer and die in ways big and small—it means that Christ's Death and Resurrection created *a way through* those realities for us. That most sacred event opened a way to not only restore us but also bring us to new and abundant life.

Lent leads us to the Cross, the stillness of the tomb, and in the end to the reorientation of our lives toward Resurrection. By taking on a new bearing and disposition firmly grounded in God's life, we no longer are bound by sin and death's destructive powers.

Prayer for Morning

Mighty One, you created us and sustain us with your love. Call me back to that love as the most important reality of my life. Help me let go of that which obstructs your way in me.

Spirit of life, come with your creative power.

Traveling Question

How can I soften my heart today?

Prayer for Evening

Mighty One, you hover over us with your creative Spirit, ready to renew what your hands have made. Reshape my heart so I may more closely reflect your image.

Spirit of life, come with your cleansing truth and love.

February 28

WEDNESDAY OF THE SECOND WEEK OF LENT

Open our hearts to the voice of your Word
and free us from the original darkness that shadows our vision.
Restore our sight that we may look upon your Son
who calls us to repentance and a change of heart.

In our fallen human condition, we don't see rightly—our vision gets clouded by self-interest. It's a proclivity that we are born with—but not one we are created to bear.

Jesus is the definitive revelation of God's truth and love for us. He not only shows us God's life; he *is* God's life—and the means by which we receive it. Seeking his presence feels a lot like listening—becoming still, quieting distraction, going within. There, in our quiet center, he speaks, for he is God's Word. With the light of his friendship, we see rightly and can make our way back to the Father.

Prayer for Morning

Almighty God, when you speak, your Word changes things by bringing life and light. Speak your Word to me today and illuminate that which shadows my vision. Grant me the ability to love you more freely.

Word of God, help me listen for you today.

Traveling Question

What darkens my vision?

Prayer for Evening

Almighty God, you made us for fullness of life with you. Restore my sight so I can look more clearly upon your Son and find him acting in my life. And in finding him, give me the courage to see how I need to change so I can share more of his love.

Word of God, call me to life.

February 29

THURSDAY OF THE SECOND WEEK OF LENT

Lord, you promised a new heaven and a new earth;
renew us daily through your Spirit.

God's creative work did not end on the day of rest we hear about in Genesis. It is ongoing. In fact, we are called to participate in it with our own labor and creativity. God's most important creative work continues in the saving work he does to reshape our hearts. We participate in that new creation as well.

We look for God's kingdom to renew our society, our culture, our systems. But before we can look for a new heaven and earth, we must first look for new hearts. Then we can roll up our sleeves and get to work.

Prayer for Morning

Creator, you continually renew your creation by joining us in love. Give me a new heart and strengthen me to join your saving work in a world that needs you.

Spirit of new life, renew me today.

Traveling Question

How can I be a source of renewal for someone today?

Prayer for Evening

Creator, your creation won't be complete until all things are united with you in perfect communion. You sent your Son, the Word of Life, as a promise that you will make all things new. Call me beyond myself, out of the tomb of brokenness and sin, and into your love.

Spirit of life, make me new.

March 1

FRIDAY OF THE SECOND WEEK OF LENT

Lord, grant us your forgiveness,
and set us free from our enslavement to sin.

Sin wounds us in three ways. Most immediately, it damages our relationship with God, other members of Christ's Body, and ourselves—even the most private sin impacts all of those connections. Second, we are doubly wounded by the shameful awareness of what we've done, which weighs us down. A third layer is that sin and its weight hinder our confidence in God's love and turn us inward—we lose sight of the horizon of God's mercy and our gaze falls downward into our own brokenness.

But we've been given good news—glad tidings of God's forgiveness. Friendship with Jesus restores us to God's love and sets us free. He is alive in our hearts in this very moment, ready for us to turn to him.

Prayer for Morning

Word of love, you came to share the Father's forgiving, merciful love, and you gave all to bring us life. Grant me your forgiveness so I can break free of my failings and walk toward your light.

Lord Jesus Christ, have mercy on me, a sinner.

Traveling Question

How can I encounter God's mercy today?

Prayer for Evening

Word of love, you lead your people to new dignity as beloved children of our Father. Free me from selfishness and small-mindedness that I may walk in your life.

Lord Jesus Christ, save me.

March 2

SATURDAY OF THE SECOND WEEK OF LENT

Teach us to be loving not only in great and exceptional moments—but above all in the ordinary events of daily life.

Every athlete wants to win—that's why they compete. The desire to win, however, is not enough for victory. It is only a feeling. If an athlete shows up to the field of play with nothing but that desire, they have no advantage because their opponent shows up equipped with the same desire. But the athlete who harnesses that desire on a cold Tuesday morning for a preseason workout turns that feeling into skill.

Habits of any kind can only be cultivated with daily practice. Wanting to be good is not enough to become good. Faithfulness is forged in day-to-day action.

Prayer for Morning

Lord Jesus, you were a craftsman and understood the value of consistent, accumulated effort. Be with me today as I seek to grow in virtue to become more like you. Keep me free from discouragement and deepen my faith and resolve.

Source of goodness, help me find you in the ordinary things of today.

Traveling Question

What small step can I take today (and tomorrow) to deepen my faithfulness?

Prayer for Evening

Lord Jesus, our Lenten journey still stretches out before us—we have weeks to go. Give me the strength to continue in my practices of self-denial, day by day.

Source of goodness, restore me this evening.

THIRD WEEK OF LENT:
LOVING OTHERS BY GIVING ALMS

March 3

THIRD SUNDAY OF LENT

May our generosity today bring joy to those in need
—in helping them may we find you.

Fr. Joe Corpora is a Holy Cross priest assigned to ministries at the University of Notre Dame. During winter and summer breaks, he travels to a Catholic Charities humanitarian center near the US-Mexico border. There, he hears confessions and anoints people, and he also prepares meals and hands out donated medicine and supplies. During one recent trip he overheard a mother asking for help arranging a bus ticket to join her husband. She was holding an infant. The night before, Fr. Joe had been out with a friend who gave him some money, so he walked with this new mother to the bus station and bought a ticket for her.

"I learned a long time ago that when someone gives me money or anything that I don't really need, the longer I hold onto it, the more reasons I will think of as to why I need the money and what I could use it for," he said. "Better to pass it on right away. Better to be a conduit for it."

In speaking with the woman, Fr. Joe learned she had gone into labor and given birth only weeks before arriving at the center. When she would rejoin her husband, he'd meet his child for the first time. She was so happy and grateful for the bus ticket.

"You cannot get into heaven without a letter of recommendation from the poor," Fr. Joe said. "I'm hoping that she will write me one someday."

Prayer for Morning

Loving Father, you are close to us in our need and call us to show your compassion to all who suffer the indignity of poverty. Open my eyes to find people in my community who lack what they need to thrive, and help me respond to their needs.

God of joy, help me find you today.

Traveling Question

How can I be generous as this day unfolds?

Prayer for Evening

Loving Father, you invite us to participate in your providing care. In doing so, we also participate in the joy of your divine life. Help me concretize my self-gift so that it makes a difference in the life of someone in need.

God of joy, open my heart.

March 4

MONDAY OF THE THIRD WEEK OF LENT

Whatever you did for one of these least brothers of mine,
you did for me.

This verse—rooted in the twenty-fifth chapter of Matthew's gospel—is the only place in the Bible where Jesus gets explicit about how to reach heaven. The standard by which we will be judged is not what we know about the faith, or how well we pray, or even what we believe about God. The only measure is how we treat people who are vulnerable.

We share life with people who are powerless because the Gospel demands this of us. We encounter Christ himself in these interactions. The exchange of gifts in that relationship—meeting each other's needs and sharing friendship—reveals God's love and makes it real.

Prayer for Morning

Loving Father, Jesus taught us to care for all who are powerless and struggle to survive. Make my heart like yours. Help me look past what I think someone deserves to see your image in them.

Lord Jesus, love of the Father, open me to the needs of others.

Traveling Question

How can I feed someone who is hungry today?

Prayer for Evening

Loving Father, in sharing life with people living on the margins, we extend your kingdom. We also receive the gift of friendship if we open ourselves to it. Help me remember that giving alms is not a one-way street—it is a practice that opens us up to an enriching relationship.

Lord Jesus, love of the Father, be with me in my need tonight.

March 5

Tuesday of the Third Week of Lent

Change our selfishness into self-giving.

This is the whole point of Lent: growing our capacity to participate in God's self-giving love, which brings new life. That growth doesn't arrive in the abstract or out of simple desire or because we believe in it. It only happens through practice—by involving our bodies in actions that bear fruit in the concrete realities of our lives.

God has placed us in a corner of the world to help him build his kingdom there. We can transform that corner if we love people there with the same love God shares with us. This is where almsgiving fits into our Lenten practice—it is a decision to change our selfish instincts through intentional self-gift that brings joy and new life.

Prayer for Morning

Lord Jesus, the Resurrection and the Life, you are faithful to our every need. Grant me a share in your new life through my Lenten practices. Help me find ways to support those in need so that I can be a source of your life and joy.

Spirit of generosity, bring me toward those who need you today.

Traveling Question

Who are the people in my community experiencing darkness and pain right now?

Prayer for Evening

Lord Jesus, the Resurrection and the Life, your way leads us toward communion. Help me reach past the things that divide us today, especially to meet people who need the touch of your love. When I find them, help me find you in our encounter.

Spirit of generosity, show me your abundance.

27

March 6

WEDNESDAY OF THE THIRD WEEK OF LENT

When you meet those who are in need of clothing,
do not turn away from them,
for they are your brothers and sisters.

Why are we called to care for people who are powerless? It is not because they are especially deserving or because they suffer nobly. It is not because you are a conservative who believes in thick social bonds or a liberal who believes in structural support for the marginalized. We are called to care for people on the margins for two reasons: they lack what they need to flourish, and they are part of our family.

Prayer for Morning

Jesus, Lord of light, in joining our humanity, you became our brother and united us as children of God, who is Love. So much of our world is organized without these bonds in mind. Help me uphold the dignity of those of us who are diminished by unjust systems.

Loving Father, form me in your love.

Traveling Question

How does my community isolate or marginalize people? What are the unwritten rules about how my city or town is organized?

Prayer for Evening

Lord of light, as evening falls, I think of those of us who lack what we need to live with dignity—whether that is electricity or food or shelter or education or loving relationships. I am also aware of my own poverty and the ways I fall short of your joy, generosity, and patience. Help me to learn that the only way to become rich in these gifts is to spend them.

Loving Father, keep me in your love.

March 7

THURSDAY OF THE THIRD WEEK OF LENT

God of mercy, let today be a day rich in good works
—a day of generosity to all we meet.

The brokenness of the world is overwhelming—there is too much for any one person to fix. In the end, we have to trust that this work of healing and saving the world is God's, and to accept that we can only take up the part that is given to us. This is work we do through small, consistent actions—by showing up and sharing what we can.

Our sphere of influence extends about twenty-five feet around us at any given time. What lives can we touch within that radius?

Prayer for Morning

God of mercy, you know every corner of this world—nothing escapes your loving gaze. You stand in even the most desolate situations, waiting for us to join your saving work. Help me integrate your love in my daily experience so that generosity becomes a way of life for me.

Providing Spirit, direct my attention and will toward ways I can give of myself today.

Traveling Question

Besides money and material help, what can I give of myself to the people I encounter today?

Prayer for Evening

God of mercy, generosity is a hallmark of your presence. Help me practice that disposition, and help me see that whatever I give is met with even more abundance.

Providing Spirit, fill my heart with the fire of your love.

March 8

FRIDAY OF THE THIRD WEEK OF LENT

Teach us to restrain our greed for earthly goods.

Our culture forms us to consider ourselves as individual economic actors, and it stokes our desire to consume. Greed isn't a stated value in our society, but that's because it is assumed—it is the water in which we swim. We need to make intentional efforts to climb out of that polluted pond to see the world differently.

We know better. As members of the Body of Christ we know that material resources are for the good of all. "The bread in your cupboard belongs to the hungry," wrote St. Basil the Great; "the coat unused in your closet belongs to the one who needs it; the shoes rotting in your closet belong to the one who has no shoes; the money which you hoard up belongs to the poor."

Prayer for Morning

God of abundance, you call us out of ourselves and toward communion with you and our brothers and sisters. Give me the courage to think and act counterculturally, to examine assumptions about what I want and to consider instead what I really need and what others need.

God of goodness, keep me grounded in communion over consumption.

Traveling Question

How can I go without a luxury or a desire today and instead provide for another?

Prayer for Evening

God of abundance, your kingdom is built on the joy of solidarity. Expand my circle of kinship to include people who are discarded and dismissed. Help me find you in their dignity and friendship.

God of goodness, help me see the world as you do.

March 9

SATURDAY OF THE THIRD WEEK OF LENT

Father, without you we can do nothing.

Jesus knew that although our spirits are willing, our flesh is weak (see Mt 26:41). Our Lenten disciplines conform us to be more responsive to God's will. But we need courage, especially to stretch beyond what's comfortable, known, and familiar. Of course, we are not alone. God sends the Holy Spirit to help us know what is right and to pursue it. And the Spirit is closer to us than we think. If we ask for help, we will be given what we need.

Prayer for Morning

Father, you provide us with everything we need—from our very lives to the desire and ability to search for you. You are so near, and yet always calling me a step further. Bend my will to your love. Shape me in your image. Give me the grace I need to follow your Son.

Spirit, draw me close and push me outward.

Traveling Question

Where do I struggle to discern God's will? How do I resist it?

Prayer for Evening

Father, you are our source of life. The goodness we yearn for comes from you, and points us back toward you wherever we find it. Grant me eagerness to do what is right in your sight, especially in the areas of my life where I hesitate or drag my feet. Help me give my life over to you.

Spirit, fill my heart and strengthen my will.

March 10

FOURTH SUNDAY OF LENT

Unless a grain of wheat falls to the ground and dies,
it remains just a grain of wheat;
but if it dies, it produces much fruit.

JOHN 12:24

Wheat has been cultivated since before the British Isles started drifting away from mainland Europe into the Atlantic. It is now a staple—wheat accounts for 20 percent of the world's caloric intake. Despite its importance in our diet, we've not been able to innovate other ways to grow it. The only way to get more wheat is by planting it in the ground.

A grain of wheat is comprised of three simple elements: the germ (or embryo) accounts for only about 3 percent of the seed—the rest is starch surrounded by a shell. When the seed is placed in soil, moisture softens the shell and activates the germ, which sends out roots and pushes a stalk upward to search for light. When it matures over the course of 120 days, one stalk can produce a head of grain with about fifty kernels. Planting one pound of wheat in the ground can generate ninety pounds of grain.

A grain of wheat is dead when it has been harvested and dried—it only comes alive when it is planted in the ground. Being buried in the cold stillness of the soil unlocks internal resources that were dormant, and the kernel takes on new life and bears a harvest many times over.

This is a good metaphor for the new pattern of living that Jesus established by his Death and Resurrection: dying opens a way to new and abundant life. Christian faith is simply living by that logic, that sacred pattern of trusting that the experience of death will bring new life. To die with Christ—even in small ways such as the self-denial of fasting—is to come to live with him. When we bury our wills in the cold, still soil, we learn we are not alone—that God was buried, too, and that the risen One will bring new life to us and we will send out roots and start reaching for light. This is the Paschal Mystery for which our Lenten journey prepares us.

Prayer for Morning

God of life, you plant your loving presence deep within us. Help me cultivate that life—to tend and keep it so that it can grow and nourish me. I cling to so many unnecessary things that distract and diminish me. Grant me strength and courage in my Lenten fast so that I can practice self-denial and learn to rely on you alone.

Risen One, your life is all I need.

Traveling Question

How can I embrace a disposition of stillness and patience in my fasting?

Prayer for Evening

God of life, you are faithful to us beyond what we can imagine. In your providence, you guide our lives toward greater and deeper love. Help me let go of the shallow pleasures and false identities that I lean on to feel secure. May my Lenten fast help me to place my life in your hands so you can multiply it and make it fruitful.

Risen One, help me embrace your Cross with hope and joy.

March 11

MONDAY OF THE FOURTH WEEK OF LENT

Father, look upon our weakness and reach out to help us
with your loving power.

We like to think about Lent as a time to roll up our sleeves and get to
work shaping up our lives with faithfulness. It's actually a time to cry
out for help—to acknowledge that we can't do this on our own. The
disciplines and practices we take up during this time are ways for us to
grow in our dependence upon God.

This dependence begins with an acknowledgment of our weakness.
We waver and are inconstant and let ourselves down. We can't seem
to escape the gravity of our own egos and keep falling back to earth.
Only God can pull us out of the orbit of self-centeredness and free us
to move toward his warmth and light.

Prayer for Morning

God of power and might, despite our weakness and inconstancy, you
never fail us with your love. Help me rely on you today so I can follow
your Son more faithfully. I know he will lead me to the hope and joy
of new life.

Holy One, be my strength.

Traveling Question

How can my fasting lead me to rely on God today?

Prayer for Evening

God of power and might, you created us for union with you and our
neighbor. In order to love more perfectly, I know I have to be willing to
set myself aside. Help me embrace fasting with joy and hope, trusting
that it will open new avenues for communion.

Holy One, be my life.

March 12

TUESDAY OF THE FOURTH WEEK OF LENT

Offer your bodies as a living sacrifice, holy and pleasing to God,
your spiritual worship.

ROMANS 12:1

Religious sacrifice of animals was the best way our Jewish ancestors in faith had to signify their faithfulness. By offering an ox or a lamb (a significant financial investment), a person was saying, "I know this is a matter of life and death, and I offer to you the best that I have."

Paul reframes that commitment by telling us to make our faithfulness even more personal by offering ourselves. We need to put our bodies on the line in order to change our hearts. Fasting is one tool we have to "offer our bodies as a living sacrifice" because it redirects the will. By making a gift of ourselves to God, we offer the best that we have.

Prayer for Morning

Mighty One, you created us in your image, and we find meaning and purpose when we make a gift of ourselves to you and others. I know that's not possible without sacrifice. Direct my fasting to selflessness so that I become more flexible in responding to you.

Lord Jesus, Lamb of God, help me die to myself today.

Traveling Question

How can I renew my Lenten fast by making a personal offering of myself to God this day?

Prayer for Evening

Mighty One, your Son's sacrifice on the Cross was the ultimate expression of self-gift. May my fasting help me embrace the crosses I've been given, so that with him I can say, "Not my will, but yours."

Lord Jesus, Lamb of God, help me share in your Resurrection.

March 13

WEDNESDAY OF THE FOURTH WEEK OF LENT

If anyone wishes to come after me,
he must deny himself, take up his cross, and follow me.

LUKE 9:23

If there were a mission statement for Lent, this would be it: deny ourselves, take up our crosses, and follow the Lord. Jesus doesn't say here that we follow him by indulging ourselves and seeking comfort and satisfaction—that's what the world calls us to do. Rather, he says that self-denial is inherent to discipleship.

That's where fasting comes in. It disrupts the things we lean on instead of God and exposes the ego. Without anything to hide behind, we have a decision to make—will we rely on God? Or will we rely on something or someone lesser?

Prayer for Morning

Lord Jesus, you call us to follow you by loving God and neighbor. To do that well, I know I have to get my ego out of the way. Help me trust that in losing myself, I will find you—and that you are all I need.

Spirit of faithfulness, give me courage and make me steadfast.

Traveling Question

What things do I lean on instead of relying on God?

Prayer for Evening

Lord Jesus, your way of self-denial opens new life for us. As we move to the Cross this Lent, help us remember we are also moving toward your Resurrection. Walk with me on this way. Help me embrace your Cross, that I might find your peace and joy.

Spirit of faithfulness, bring me life.

March 14

THURSDAY OF THE FOURTH WEEK OF LENT

Loving Redeemer, through your passion teach us self-denial,
strengthen us against evil and adversity, and increase our hope
—and so make us ready to celebrate your resurrection.

The Resurrection changed the bounds of reality for us—it changed our
story. When he was raised from the dead, Jesus opened a way through
death for us, making the Cross a symbol of hope which the world will
never understand. Without faith, suffering and death are only darkness.
But with Jesus, our darkness becomes light, weakness becomes strength,
and death becomes life. Our Lenten disciplines of self-denial are ways
to practice embracing the Cross, to increase our willingness to let go of
anything that is incompatible with the one necessary thing: God's life.

Prayer for Morning

Savior of the world, your Cross is a source of life for us. Your way reveals
our own crosses where we find deeper union with you. Meet me in my
Lenten fast so that I can more clearly recognize you with me in the
crosses I must carry.

Jesus, my hope, strengthen me today.

Traveling Question

How will I experience the Cross today—and how can I meet Jesus there?

Prayer for Evening

Savior of the world, your Resurrection is a source of hope for us. Your
faithful love never fails me—it is wider and deeper than anything that
threatens me. Help me look for your love above anything else in my life.

Jesus, my hope, I trust in you.

March 15

FRIDAY OF THE FOURTH WEEK OF LENT

May we bear the wounds of your Son in our bodies,
for through his body he gave us life.

We think of Lent as a season of spiritual preparation, but it is no less a season that involves our bodies because they are united with our souls. Easter promises us that we not only receive spiritual life from God when we die to ourselves, but that we will also receive physical life from God in the resurrection of the dead. So faith is more than an idea, more than a consoling feeling in our hearts—it involves our flesh and bones.

Jesus made faith real on the Cross—he didn't just preach self-sacrificing love; he embodied it. Fasting is one way we join Jesus's faith—in making sacrifice real, we prepare for the redemption of our bodies.

Prayer for Morning

Lord Jesus, through your suffering and death, you never let go of love. Through the humiliation of betrayal, the cruelty of scourging, and even the agony of crucifixion, you remained faithful to love. May my fasting strip away anything that compromises my ability to love as fully as you did.

Father, deepen my faith.

Traveling Question

How can I make my faith more than an intellectual assent today?

Prayer for Evening

Lord Jesus, your love for us led to your wounding and death. God's love for us led to your Resurrection. As I move through this Lenten season, help me bear my wounds with your faithfulness and love, trusting that God will raise me to new and abundant life.

Father, expand my hope.

March 16

Saturday of the Fourth Week of Lent

Lord, guide us in your gentle mercy,
for left to ourselves we cannot do your will.

Plants know how to stretch for the sun—they bend their stalks and leaves to reach for the nourishing daylight. God's mercy leads us in the same way. Once we have experienced a taste of it, we stretch for more.

The work of Lent—the real work we are doing through all of our Lenten disciplines—is to clear away anything that is getting in the way of God's life in us. If we are moving too fast, we don't notice God's warmth and light. Fasting slows us down and puts our desires in order. It sharpens our spiritual senses to perceive and live in God's mercy—to hunger for God alone.

Prayer for Morning

Merciful Father, you call us to return to you in this season of Lent. As I find nourishment in your love, help me remain with you—to slow down and let go of anything that falsifies your image in me—so that I can radiate your presence to others.

Spirit of the living God, guide me to do your will today.

Traveling Question

How will God invite me to live in his mercy today?

Prayer for Evening

Merciful Father, you are our source of life. May my efforts this Lent reflect my dependence on you. When I try to work my way back to you, I get off track and out of balance. Help me turn my life over to you—to see you acting within my very desire to return to you.

Spirit of the living God, bring me back to you.

FIFTH WEEK OF LENT:
UNION WITH GOD IN PRAYER

March 17

FIFTH SUNDAY OF LENT

Jesus, you feed and heal our souls; come to strengthen us.

On the night of April 4, 2022, Sr. Suellen Tennyson—former international leader of the Marianites of Holy Cross—was abducted from the mission where she was serving in Burkina Faso, West Africa. Armed rebels blindfolded and gagged the eighty-three-year-old nun and took her by motorcycle to a hidden location. She didn't have her medications or glasses or even a pair of shoes.

Over the five months of her captivity, she suffered from isolation and neglect—she contracted malaria and lost twenty pounds. She was forced to sleep outside on the ground under a small shelter made of branches. She had no idea where she was, nor how long she would be held.

Without books, she relied on the prayers and Bible passages she had memorized, including the words of the Mass and the Rosary. "Prayer sustained me," she told the newspaper of the New Orleans archdiocese, *The Clarion Herald*. "That was the thing that kept me going because I had nothing.

"I had many conversations with God," she said. "I would say, 'Okay, God, what's your word to me today at this moment?' Sometimes it was a Scripture passage or a story from Scripture. But, after a while, it was just messages to me. And the one that stayed with me the longest was 'peaceful patience. You need to be peacefully patient.'"

The dialogue Sr. Suellen speaks of here is indicative of a rich prayer life. Rote prayer formed the bedrock of her conversations with God, and then she reached beyond that formal language to simply share her life with God—and she received the consolation of God's presence in return. At one point, she asked in prayer if God had abandoned her, and heard God telling her in reply, "Suellen, I have loved you with an everlasting love. I have called you, and you are mine."

Prayer was the only resource Sr. Suellen could draw on to survive—everything else was out of her control. So she shared her life with God, using what she could remember from our tradition and her own words, and found that God was faithful to her—that she was not alone.

Prayer for Morning

God, our Father, you are closer to us than we can imagine, ready to share life with us. Help me share my life with you. When I don't have the words, grant me a sense of your presence, and if I cannot feel you near, grant me faith to trust your promise of faithfulness.

Faithful One, speak into my life today.

Traveling Question

When and how will I turn to God in prayer today to share my life with him?

Prayer for Evening

God, our Father, you sustain us with your love and order our lives toward union with you. I know prayer is the means of communication between us—but even more than what I want to say is this desire I have to be near you, to come alive in your presence. Please draw close to me in this prayer.

Faithful One, be with me.

March 18

MONDAY OF THE FIFTH WEEK OF LENT

When you pray, go to your inner room, close the door,
and pray to your Father in secret.

MATTHEW 6:6

Prayer is a personal exchange with God—it is where, as St. Francis de Sales said, "heart speaks to heart." That exchange in private prayer is nourished by our exchanges with God in public prayer and worship, but there's an indispensable connection that can only happen in the stillness of an interior room where we meet God.

Our prayer practice during Lent requires that we go to this interior room often and shut the door to other distractions. That's what we are doing together with this booklet—giving our time and attention to God and listening for his presence in reply.

Prayer for Morning

Living God, you created our hearts to echo with your voice. I want to hear you speaking into my life. Help me turn to you in prayer—in listening for you, I know I will find you walking with me through even the small moments of my day.

Spirit of holiness, quiet my heart.

Traveling Question

Where can I find a few moments of silence today?

Prayer for Evening

Living God, you hold each of us as your beloved children. I know your love is deep enough to carry my past, present, and future. I turn it all over to you and rest in your mercy.

Spirit of holiness, bring me to the Father.

March 19

SOLEMNITY OF ST. JOSEPH

Joseph went and dwelt in a town called Nazareth,
so that what had been spoken through the prophets might be
fulfilled, "He will be called a Nazorean."
MATTHEW 2:23

Joseph's feast day fittingly falls during Lent every year because he was a man of action. No words are recorded from him in the Bible—we remember him for what he did, not what he said.

From the moment he met Mary, Joseph's life took a very different course than he could have possibly imagined. From their marriage and her pregnancy, to fleeing to Egypt, to the strange gifts of his son, Joseph would have had to rethink his life at every turn. He probably had to let go of what he thought his life would be like and embrace the new direction in which God was leading. He was faithful. Perhaps being a craftsman reinforced a disposition of quiet strength.

We think of Joseph as a carpenter, but the biblical word for his trade is closer to a stonemason—someone who built homes. Joseph knew how important it was to show up and go about your work every day. The structures he built would have taken weeks or maybe months to complete. Every morning, he showed up and gave his sweat and blood to projects—even on corners and joints that no one would ever see. He would have returned home covered with dust and sweat stains. People who shook his hand would have been impressed with his grip.

We might assume that Joseph mentored Jesus in the same trade. For years, they likely rose at the same hour, packed food and water, gathered tools, and set out for the job site as the city was coming awake. Perhaps Jesus wore the label Nazorean with pride, knowing that though this mid-sized city was not a center of power or trade, it was an everyday town full of people who took pride in their work.

We who follow the Nazorean take on the quiet faithfulness he likely learned from Joseph.

Prayer for Morning

Lord Jesus, Joseph taught you the virtues of a craft—honesty, integrity, and hard work. Build within me these same virtues. In these last days of our Lenten journey, help me continue to show up and to strive for faithfulness.

St. Joseph, pray for me that I may reflect your quiet strength.

Traveling Question

How can I show up for the people in my life today?

Prayer for Evening

Lord Jesus, Joseph taught you the virtues of being a husband and father. In watching him, you witnessed self-giving love that provided a shelter for you and Mary. Grant me the same generosity so I may also provide the same kind of love to those who are closest to me.

St. Joseph, pray for me so I may reflect your faithfulness.

March 20

WEDNESDAY OF THE FIFTH WEEK OF LENT

Teach us the meaning and value of creation—
so that we may join its voice to ours as we sing your praise.

Praise is a form of prayer that leaps out of us. The beauty of the natural world moves us, whether it's a grand sunset or the intricacy of the joints on the legs of a beetle. When these moments lift our hearts, it's just a small additional turn to lift them to the Lord.

Praise restores us to our rightful place in the world—it acknowledges that God is Creator and we are his creatures. That right order puts us in harmony with the world—we can sit firmly in our place in the universe, which is small but mightily loved.

Prayer for Morning

Loving Creator, all creation sings your name. Help me to know my place in this expansive universe, and to find you right there next to me, calling me deeper into the mystery of your creative love.

Spirit of goodness and beauty, help me sing God's praise.

Traveling Question

Where will I find beauty today?

Prayer for Evening

Loving Creator, you have imbued creation with your grandeur. As wide and beautiful as this world is, you have created each of us with an interior landscape that is even more grand. Help me explore it, so I can discover your handiwork in the core of my being.

Spirit of goodness and beauty, lift my heart to the Lord.

March 21

THURSDAY OF THE FIFTH WEEK OF LENT

Teach us to seek the bread of everlasting life—
the bread that is your gift.

Where do we seek nourishment? How do we fill our deepest hungers? All too often we attempt to mask our desires with distractions and shallow pleasures. For a time, we are sated, but then we find that we are hungry again.

Lent is a time to explore these desires, rather than patch them up. This restlessness we feel is inexhaustible—it is a bottomless hole—so it does us no good to keep throwing things into it. But we can recognize that yearning for what it is: hunger for God. If we turn to God to fill our need, we will find an inexhaustible source of life. He can make us whole.

Prayer for Morning

Our Father, you freely feed us with finest wheat—with the very Body of your Son. Help me explore my hungers, and to turn to you when I begin to feel anxious or discouraged. You are aware of my every need, and will provide everything for me.

Bread of Life, nourish me with your love.

Traveling Question

How can I turn to God today when I feel dissatisfied and restless?

Prayer for Evening

Our Father, you send us bread from heaven to sustain us on our journey to you. The daily bread you offer is enough for our next step. Help me move forward with trust that you will provide me tomorrow's bread when I arrive there.

Bread of Life, nourish me with your life.

March 22

FRIDAY OF THE FIFTH WEEK OF LENT

*Pour your love into the hearts of all who share
the one bread of life.*

This booklet of reflections began with a promise to connect readers around the world in prayer. How is this possible?

If we become one with God in prayer, we become one with everyone else who is one with God. More precisely, we are all members of one body—and Christ is the source of our unity. In becoming human, and in his suffering, Death, and Resurrection, we are made whole again and united in the divine life of the Trinity. Our discipleship puts us in relationship with everyone else who is following Christ. And because he is the Lord of space and time, that fellowship spans the ages. By following the Bread of Life, we are nourished at the same table and forever joined in the communion with the risen Christ.

Prayer for Morning

Bread of Life, you gave your body to bring us to the Father; you continue to feed us with your body in the Eucharist. Break me open and pour your love into me so I may know and serve others.

Spirit of unity, help me draw others to God's table today.

Traveling Question

Whom can I ask for help in discipleship who shares a history with me—a grandparent, ancestor, saint?

Prayer for Evening

Bread of Life, you sustain us on our journey to the Father. May your Body keep me faithful and strong enough to walk with you to the Cross, through the tomb, and into new life.

Spirit of unity, draw me together with others following Christ's way.

March 23

SATURDAY OF THE FIFTH WEEK OF LENT

Help us to receive good things from your bounty
with a deep sense of gratitude.

Prayer opens our eyes to see God providing for us. It helps us see God walking with us and gives us what we need to remain faithful. Prayer changes us from living in scarcity, competition, and isolation to being surrounded by abundance. It does not remove the Cross—but it does help us find a way through its darkness and pain.

We didn't create our own way in this world—rather, we receive life and purpose from the hand of the Lord. Our gratitude acknowledges the One who created us, redeems us, and makes us holy.

Prayer for Morning

God of providence, you do great things for us and holy is your name. As I head into the mysteries of Holy Week, keep me anchored in gratitude for all you do for me. As I join your Son in turning toward the Cross, I give thanks for your promise of new life.

Spirit of abundance, deepen my awareness of how God is acting in my life.

Traveling Question

How is God providing for me today?

Prayer for Evening

God of providence, you come to our help and show us your strength. Save me from myself and from all that threatens my faith and hope. Grow my love for you and others.

Spirit of abundance, deepen my gratitude for how God is acting in my life.

March 24

Palm Sunday

The Lord GOD is my help,
therefore I am not disgraced.

The History Channel has a show called *Alone* where ten people are taken into the wilderness of British Columbia to see how long they can survive through the fall and winter. The person who survives the longest wins half a million dollars. In the first days, the greatest danger is bears. But as the first weeks pass, not scavenging enough food becomes a greater threat. For those who manage to gather enough to eat for months, however, the greatest obstacle is simply being alone.

They get lonely, of course, but the isolation brings out something deeper. Without other people or the noise of life or the demands of work, the contestants are forced to confront themselves. In the silence of the forest, the only sounds are dripping rain and a snapping fire. Each one of them speaks about memories and failed relationships and regrets, and how they can't escape them. They are haunted by shame, and many can't take it—they call for rescue and go home.

At the outset, the central conflict in the show appears to be between people and nature, but the real drama unfolds within each contestant.

As we enter Holy Week, we step into this same sort of drama. Palm Sunday shows us conflict and triumph ahead, but the real action happens within. The key is to attend to the interior life of Jesus through this week. We can walk with him—from his entry into Jerusalem, to Calvary, and through the tomb into the garden, joining our own stories, our journey of the last year, to his story. More than it is about recalling

Christ's Death and Resurrection, Holy Week is about joining our lives to the Cross and clinging to the hope of the Resurrection.

However imperfect our Lent has been this year, we must not allow shame to get in the way. In the celebration of the Sacred Triduum that awaits us at the end of this week, we are plunged again into the Paschal Mystery wherein Christ claims us anew and brings us to new life. He lets nothing stand in the way of our identity and ultimate destiny as his beloved, and members of his Body, the Church.

Prayer for Morning

Jesus our Savior, you experienced the adulation of crowds and the betrayal or your closest friends. Through the highs and lows we remember this week, you kept your eyes on the Father and were not moved from your faithfulness. Help me hold fast to his love as you did.

God, come to my assistance.

Traveling Question

Is there anything that stands in the way of my making a full-hearted journey with Jesus through Holy Week? How can I confront that shame and hand it over to him?

Prayer for Evening

Jesus our Savior, from your triumphal entry into Jerusalem to the agony of the Cross to the glory of the empty tomb, you trusted in God's power to save. Deepen my faith so I may live with the confidence that nothing can harm me if I am God's. Help me trust in God's saving power as well.

Lord, make haste to help me.

March 25

MONDAY OF HOLY WEEK

God proves his love for us in that while we were still sinners,
Christ died for us.

ROMANS 5:8

God is not intimidated by cruelty or violence or even death—like the rain, God's love descends upon all of us. Jesus did not come only to good people. He committed to all of us.

The same faithfulness and generosity are on display in Holy Week: Jesus pours his life out for all of us—from the stranger who helps carry his cross to the soldiers who spit on him. We approach the Cross, too, with our own mixed hearts. We cannot earn this love, nor can we do anything to become unworthy of it, for this is who God is: self-gift.

Prayer for Morning

Lord Jesus, glory of the Father, you came to live among us—even to become our servant. You humbled yourself, even to humiliation and death, because this is who you are: God's self-giving love in the flesh. Help me to follow you, and in following you, to become like you.

God of love, help me give of myself today.

Traveling Question

How might I love as God does?

Prayer for Evening

Lord Jesus, glory of the Father, you saw the worst in us and did not abandon us. You could have turned away and left us to what we deserve: death. Instead, you revealed a way through our darkest moments. Deepen my faith and grant me a share in the fullness of your life.

God of love, bring me to new life.

March 26

TUESDAY OF HOLY WEEK

In their trials, enable your faithful people to share in your passion—
and so reveal in their lives your saving power.

Jesus suffered the worst: the apparent failure of his life's work, betrayal from his closest friends, public humiliation, agonizing torture, and cruel death.

When suffering comes our way, the Lord arrives with it—he's there to walk with us right to the end and beyond. He will never fail us. When we hand ourselves over and suffer with Jesus, we share even more deeply in his gift of self, which means we also share more deeply in the glory of his divine life. Like him, we become a light shining in darkness.

Prayer for Morning

Light of the World, in baptism our lives are patterned after your self-giving love. Help me to live as you did: faithful to the Father and full of love for others. In my trials, may I join you on my own way of the cross.

Spirit of the living God, save me.

Traveling Question

How can I join my life to Jesus's suffering today?

Prayer for Evening

Light of the World, when you came to live among us, you consented to die with us. I know your friendship won't prevent me from experiencing pain and death, but it does give me the opportunity to live like you through that suffering—and thus become a sign of your love for others.

Spirit of the living God, sustain me.

March 27

WEDNESDAY OF HOLY WEEK

You made the cross the tree of life—
give its fruit to those reborn in baptism.

Hopefully, Lent has prepared us to enter the mystery of Jesus's suffering, Death, and Resurrection. We've walked the last forty days with those who will be baptized and received into full communion with us at the Easter Vigil. Their presence calls us to renewal by embracing the Cross of Jesus and the promise of the Resurrection.

On this last full day of Lent, we remember that we no longer need to fear death, either in the myriad ways we are asked to die to ourselves every day or in the final step we take into the next world.

Prayer for Morning

Loving Creator, you made the wood of the cross into a living tree that bears the fruit of hope. Grant me greater hope in your Son's Resurrection so I can live with more resilience, purpose, and generosity—and share this hope with others living in darkness.

Living Savior, keep me close to your way.

Traveling Question

What fruit does faith grow in my life? How might it feed others?

Prayer for Evening

Loving Creator, through the gift of baptism, you allow us to see life differently than the world does. In the face of adversity, my instincts turn to self-protection and defensiveness. Help me confront whatever threatens me with generosity, patience, and hope born of the confidence that you have already conquered the world.

Living Savior, help me live in your victory.

March 28

HOLY THURSDAY

The Lord said, "Israel I will feed with the finest wheat,
I will satisfy them with honey from the rock."

PSALM 81:17

At sundown today, Lent ends. Our journey has us poised to plunge into the mystery of Christ's Passion, Death, and Resurrection as we celebrate the Easter Triduum. We will listen once again to the gospel stories of the Last Supper, the agony in the Garden of Gethsemane, the trial of Jesus before Pilate and the Jewish leaders of Jerusalem, his death, and the story of the women at the empty tomb.

Now, the Church takes up all that we've been given these last forty days and we bring it together to the Lord's table where it will once again be made our heavenly food, the Body and Blood of our Eucharistic Lord.

Prayer for Morning

Faithful God, you are always good to us. Bring me into the communion of your life with the Son and the Spirit, and transform me to be good for others.

Jesus, Bread of Life, bring me to your table, feed me with your Body and Blood.

Traveling Question

How has God fed me this Lent?

Prayer for Evening

Faithful God, you did not abandon your Son in his suffering and death. Do not abandon me in my trials. I look to you for nourishment. Deepen my faith, grant me hope, and expand my love.

Jesus, Bread of Life, I watch and pray with you.

March 29

GOOD FRIDAY

God has reconciled us to himself through Christ.
2 CORINTHIANS 5:18

God wants nothing more than union with each one of us—so much so that he became one with us. He gave us the best of himself: his only Son. Jesus healed and taught us—and for that he was abused and crucified. Yet Father, Son, and Spirit still cling to us.

We continue to turn away from God out of our foolish desires, willful ignorance, and shallow selfishness. But even in our sinfulness God reaches us—taking up our rejection and overwhelming it with mercy and love. What more could God do to reveal his love for us? Though at times we turn away from him, we can *always* return—Christ waits with arms spread wide, ready to save us.

Prayer for Morning

Lord Jesus Christ, you are our way, truth, and light. We've been walking with you these past forty days. Today, we go to the Cross with you. Help me to accept what is keeping me from you and to offer it to God, trusting in his power to save.

Jesus, help me take up my cross.

Traveling Question

What do I most need God to save me from?

Prayer for Evening

Lord Jesus Christ, you will not allow our sinfulness to keep us away from the Father. Give me the courage to ask for your healing and reconciliation in my life, for you are willing to grant it if I am willing to embrace your Cross.

Jesus, I empty myself with you.

March 30

HOLY SATURDAY

Christ our Savior,
your sorrowing Mother stood by you at your death and burial—
in our sorrows may we share in your suffering.

Today we recall the silence of death and meditate on the grief of those who loved and followed Jesus. Mary was one of these. She stayed with Jesus through all of his miracles and teaching, his confrontations with power, and his trial and torture and death. When he suffered, her love for him allowed her to meet his eyes. When she buried him, her faith allowed her to sink into the depths of grief without giving in to despair. Mary is Our Lady of Sorrows, and when we suffer, she stands near. When we are entombed, she mourns and waits for us, to bring us hope.

Prayer for Morning

Our Lady of Sorrows, your love for us is as constant as it is for your Son. Stand with me in my brokenness, and help me receive the hope that kept you strong.

Mother of Hope, pray for me and those I love.

Traveling Question

Today, we recall those who have died and await the resurrection—what are the names of the departed I remember and pray for today?

Prayer for Evening

Our Lady of Sorrows, the suffering and death of your beloved Son did not cause you to question your faith in the Mighty One. That trust was vindicated on Easter when God's creative work broke into our world in a new way. Pray that my faith and trust may deepen as well, and help me grow in hope for the newness of God's life.

Mother of Hope, help me grow in faith.

March 31

EASTER SUNDAY: HE IS RISEN! ALLELUIA!

God our Father, by raising Christ your Son
you conquered the power of death
and opened for us the way to eternal life.
Let our celebration today raise us up and renew our lives
by the Spirit that is within us.

A month after their honeymoon in 2008, Chiara and Enrico Corbella Petrillo discovered they were expecting a child. As the pregnancy developed, however, doctors discovered that their child was growing with abnormalities that would make survival impossible. Their daughter lived less than an hour after birth.

Months later, Chiara again became pregnant. Once again, the couple was devastated to discover that a completely different genetic abnormality afflicted this child. Their son survived less than an hour after birth.

"In our marriage, the Lord gave us two special children," Chiara reflected, "but he asked us to accompany them only until their birth. He gave us the opportunity to embrace them, have them baptized, and then entrust them into the hands of the Father, all with a peace and joy that we had never experienced before."

Chiara's third pregnancy arrived with a clean bill of health for the child. But five months in, Chiara developed a lesion on her tongue, which was diagnosed as cancer. She decided to forego treatment to protect the pregnancy, losing the ability to speak and swallow; she began to lose her sight as well. After her son was born healthy, the chemotherapy was not enough to stem the spread of the disease. Chiara died in 2012 at the age of twenty-eight. Her cause for canonization was opened in 2018.

Chiara was familiar with death—she experienced more than her share of sorrow. In her illness, her friends saw her struggle with anxiety and fear on top of the pain and nausea. But she believed in God's faithfulness—the same faithful love that raised Jesus from the dead. That faith gave her hope—even joy—and the certainty that mortal death is not our end.

At the funeral for her daughter, Chiara and Enrico handed out memorial cards with the phrase, "We are born never to die."

Prayer for Morning

Risen Lord, in your rising you conquered death and opened new life for us. Help me walk in your way, which enables me to live without fear and love without reservation. Help me to rejoice in the gift of new life you offer.

God of life, raise me up.

Traveling Question

How will hope and joy mark my life in this Easter season?

Prayer for Evening

Risen Lord, you make all things new. I give you thanks for making me new through the mystery of your Cross and Resurrection. Help me commit to your love in the weeks ahead, and to find ways to bring your peace and joy to those who need good news.

God of life, renew me!

Founded in 1865 by Fr. Edward Sorin, CSC, **Ave Maria Press** is an apostolate of the Congregation of Holy Cross, United States Province of Priests and Brothers. Ave is a nonprofit Catholic publishing ministry that serves the spiritual and formative needs of the Church and its schools, institutions, and ministers; Christian individuals and families; and others seeking spiritual nourishment.

Ave remains one of the oldest continually operating Catholic publishing houses in the country and a leader in publishing Catholic high school religion textbooks, ministry resources, and books on prayer and spirituality.

In the tradition of Holy Cross, Ave is committed, as an educator in the faith, to help people know, love, and serve God and to spread the gospel of Jesus Christ through books and other resources.

Ave Maria Press perpetuates Fr. Sorin's vision to honor Mary and provide an important outlet for good Catholic writing.

AVE

AVE MARIA PRESS

Founded in 1865, Ave Maria Press,
a ministry of the Congregation of
Holy Cross, is a Catholic publishing
company that serves the spiritual and
formative needs of the Church and its
schools, institutions, and ministers;
Christian individuals and families; and
others seeking spiritual nourishment.

For a complete listing of titles from

Ave Maria Press

Sorin Books

Forest of Peace

Christian Classics

visit www.avemariapress.com

AVE MARIA PRESS
Notre Dame, IN
A Ministry of the United States Province of Holy Cross